Original title:
Pothos and Poetry

Copyright © 2025 Creative Arts Management OÜ
All rights reserved.

Author: Jasper Montgomery
ISBN HARDBACK: 978-1-80581-761-1
ISBN PAPERBACK: 978-1-80581-288-3
ISBN EBOOK: 978-1-80581-761-1

Green Alchemy of Expression

In a pot on the sill, a green vine does grow,
Twisting and turning, putting on a show.
It sneezes and giggles in the morning light,
Chasing the dust bunnies, ready for flight.

The leaves whisper secrets to the sun's warm rays,
They tell silly tales of their leafy plays.
With each little bounce, they flip and they flop,
Creating a dance that just will not stop!

Caught in a tangle, oh, what a sight,
A leaf wraps around a pen, oh so tight!
Writing down jokes about water and soil,
Making each moment a sprightly recoiling.

The pot's full of laughter, the soil's full of glee,
While squirrels and birds share a chuckle, you see!
With roots deep in humor, they plan their next prank,
In this world of green, we all join the tank!

Lyrical Trails of Green

In gardens where the shadows stroll,
Nature hums a giggling roll.
Leaves dance like they've lost the plot,
Whispering secrets, oh, what a lot!

With every twist, they laugh and spin,
Reminding us to shed our skin.
A leaf, a rhyme, a loopy chase,
In this green maze, there's no dull face!

Ink and Ivy Intertwined

In corners where the wild things grow,
A scribble spritzed with a funny show.
Tipsy vines, they curl and creep,
Shouting from the paper heap!

Words tangle like a playful jest,
Ink and leaves in a leafy fest.
Wordplay blooms with a chuckle loud,
Nature's light makes the poets proud!

Tendrils of Expression

A frilly leaf, a cheeky grin,
Swaying gently in a merry spin.
Hooks and curls, they tell a tale,
Of giggles lost on a windy sail.

With every twist, a pun appears,
In the green, we shed our fears.
Spill the ink, let it splay,
Funny tendrils lead the way!

Green Verses in the Sunlight

Sunlight dances on leafy prose,
Tickling words under verdant bows.
With laughter echoing through the air,
Every rhyme slicks back a strand of hair!

Dappled shadows skip and leap,
A chorus of giggles till we weep.
In this bright patch, let's be free,
Writing verses with a growing glee!

Flourish of the Inked Heart

Inked heart dances, quills in flight,
A scribbled joke, a silly plight.
Leaves laugh softly, whispers in green,
Puns sprout up, so fresh and seen.

Words take root, with humor sown,
As vines twirl round a prose-filled throne.
Each line a branch, a quirky twist,
In this lively forest, we can't resist.

Clarity Among the Climbing Foliage

Climbing high, those leafy shares,
Jokes entwined with twisty pairs.
A leafy grin, in sunlight's gaze,
Punchlines sprout in tangled ways.

Through the greenery, laughter grows,
With every turn, a whimsy flows.
A rhyme, a chuckle, all in the chase,
Nature's humor, a leafy embrace.

Verses from the Leafy Canopy

Beneath the leaves, a playful swell,
Where cheeky rhymes in darkness dwell.
Each branch a word, in leafy laugh,
Scribbling joy on nature's graph.

With every rustle, a jest appears,
Tickling ears while quenching fears.
The canopy's giggles, a soft delight,
As verses peek through, and take to flight.

The Poetry of Nature's Embrace

In the embrace of sun-kissed boughs,
Words wear smiles, taking bows.
A cheerful jest flutters by,
In nature's script, oh my, oh my!

Leaves nod along, each punchline bright,
Nature scripts a silly night.
Beneath the stars, giggles ignite,
As leafy tales take playful flight.

The Unwritten Canopy

In a jungle of thoughts, vines intertwine,
Ideas dangle like grapes on a line.
I ponder my words, then trip on the floor,
Watch as my muse crawls out the back door.

Each leaf a giggle, a rustling jest,
At this leafy party, I'm far from the best.
My rhymes get tangled like hair in a breeze,
I laugh at my chaos, oh please, do not tease.

Threads of Green Thought

With leaves as my guides, I venture and sway,
Twisting my thoughts in a playful array.
Why is my pen dancing on this fine page?
Caught in the whimsy, it's starting to rage!

I sip on dew drops, disguised as my drink,
Each word I scribble leads me to think.
Is that a new pet, or my vivid design?
Oh dear, it's a vine! Now it's eating my wine!

Bards of the Leafy Realm

In the realm of green, where laughter takes flight,
The bards craft their verses all day and all night.
One plant spills rhymes while the other tells jokes,
I can hardly keep up, and my side nearly chokes!

The ferns have opinions on love and despair,
While succulents giggle and toss through the air.
Oh, what a life, the puns never cease,
Join me in wormwood, let's party in peace.

Harmonies in Hues

Colors collide like a paint-splattered fight,
As leaves hum a ballad, in morning's first light.
I dance with my words as they spin through the air,
And laugh at my lack of poetic flair.

Each hue has a joke, a quip to bestow,
While my sentences waltz, oh, where will they go?
In the garden of humor, I frolic and play,
Finding joy in the mishaps that come my way.

Thoughts in the Leafy Canopy

In the green above, ideas play,
Like squirrels who forgot the way.
They leap and spin in endless chase,
While I just watch, a smiling face.

The vines twist round, oh what a sight,
They weave my thoughts both day and night.
I wonder if they ever tire,
Or if they're just fueled by desire.

Growing Instincts

With tendrils stretching, they reach for fun,
Every little leaf a race begun.
They giggle as they bump and slide,
And in their dance, I feel the pride.

Do roots have dreams beneath the ground?
Perhaps they're here to fool around.
With every wiggle, twist, and shout,
I join their joy, there's no doubt.

Green Dreams of Distant Echoes

In shades of green, their whispers grow,
As silly thoughts begin to flow.
Each leaf a giggle, a winking eye,
In morning light, they dance and sigh.

Echoes bounce from vine to vine,
Spreading laughter, oh how divine!
I'd join their games, but alas, I'm stuck,
Watching closely without much luck.

A Tangle of Ideas

A tangle here, a twisty thought,
Woven humor, joy is caught.
From tangled vines, a riddle grows,
Can plants really crack all the jokes?

In every curl and every twist,
I find a punchline that I missed.
So let them laugh, the green brigade,
In their leafy world, I'm happily swayed.

Enchanted Greenery in Lines

In a pot, a vine does twirl,
With twists and curls, it gives a whirl.
It yells, "Hey there! Give me sun!"
And I just laugh; it's all in fun.

Leaves like smiles that wink and glow,
Dancing in the breeze; oh, what a show!
Whispering secrets to the air,
It's the plant that knows how to care.

Each leaf a scribble in my mind,
A jolly tale of the green kind.
"Don't forget to water me!"
Its cheeky voice, a melody.

In corners bright, it spreads delight,
Painting shadows with laughter, light.
As poets jot strange, silly rhymes,
This leafy muse ticks off the times.

Resilient Thoughts in the Shade

Beneath the shade, the green ones sigh,
"We're thriving, we're crafty, give us a try!"
They stretch and reach in playful ways,
Creating riddles that brighten days.

In pots they plot a leafy game,
Whispering jokes that can't be tamed.
"Oh human, come, let's make a mess!"
In tangles of vines, they laugh and jest.

A leaf fell down, a gentle thud,
We joked it rolled like it's in the mud.
"Watch out, there's dirt!" they tease with glee,
Each rustle sounds like pure poetry.

Under the sun, they grow so bold,
Filling hearts with stories untold.
These greens have the wit, a natural flair,
Who needs a quill when they're already there?

The Art of Flourishing Lines

With twining roots, they sway and twist,
These humble greens can't be missed.
"Oh, look at me, I'm quite the sight!"
They giggle softly in morning light.

In every nook, they settle down,
Adorning spaces with their crown.
"Not just a plant, I'm quite the catch!"
Oh, the ways they've learned to hatch!

Leaves like verses, crinkled and bright,
Scribbling stories under the light.
"Pot me maybe?" they call in jest,
For every home needs a leafy guest.

Their laughter drips like morning dew,
While flourishing tales in green ensue.
In secret corners, jokes unfold,
Artful charms from young to old.

Verses Wrapped in Green

In tendrils curled, they find their way,
Squirrels stop by for a giggling play.
"Who wrote this line?" they chirp with glee,
Wrapped in greens, what fun to be!

With every leaf, a story spins,
Whispering laughter beneath the skins.
"Let's change the world, one leaf at a time!"
In tangled antics, they craft their rhyme.

Each sprout a plot twist, bold and grand,
As they beckon you with a leafy hand.
"Join us here in this leafy retreat!"
Where humor blooms, life tastes so sweet.

So toss your pen, let nature write,
For green dreams twirl in the sunlight.
With a chuckle and a gentle sigh,
These leafy jests will never die.

Leafy Sonnets

In a pot that dreams all day,
Leaves are having tea, hooray!
They giggle and dance, quite absurd,
Whispering secrets, oh so blurred.

A leaf with shades of green so bright,
Claims it can fly, oh what a sight!
Another guffaws, 'Are you for real?'
His charm is such, it's hard to conceal.

The watering can joins in the spree,
Joking of drops and a wild spree.
A humor fest in a tiny space,
Where sunlight's laughter lights the place.

Every twist and turn they make,
Spreading joy for all our sake.
In this leafy lounge, so divine,
Is nature's punchline, oh so fine!

Nature's Lines of Verse

In the garden where the wild things dwell,
A seed told a joke; it rang like a bell.
The daisies rolled over, they laughed so loud,
Even the cacti joining the crowd.

A mischievous breeze made flowers sway,
"Hey dudes, stop moving! It's not your day!"
But petals just giggled, swaying cheekily,
Finding the rhythm, all breezily free.

Oh, the soil creaked, a funny old chap,
"I'm just trying to nap, take a long map!"
Roots tangled together, a comedy show,
Beneath all the humor, they bloomed just so.

Nature's whimsy is hard to outpace,
With every green laugh, we join in the race.
So raise a glass, let laughter unfurl,
In this verdant world, give joy a twirl!

The Language of Lushness

In a jungle gym of blossoms bright,
A squawking parrot took to flight.
He said, "Why did the fern cross the way?
To leaf its worries, come what may!"

Butterflies flit with a giggle or two,
"Did you hear that, it's a funny hue?"
With dance on the wind, they twirl and glide,
In this nature's build, there's nowhere to hide.

Worms in the mulch share tales of delight,
"Did you hear about the bee who took flight?
He buzzed so hard and fell on his nose,
Now he wears pollen like a fancy prose!"

Under the sun, all creatures conspire,
To make each moment fun, never tires.
So take a cue from the blooms all around,
In this lush universe, joy can abound!

Verses in the Verdant

In a patch of green where humor thrives,
Frogs croak jokes as the laughter dives.
They plan a show near the lily pad,
With a punchline so good, it's never sad.

The grasses sway, they join the choir,
"Why did the daisy feel so higher?"
It giggled and spun, "I dug my roots deep,
Now I'm a star, just watch as I leap!"

Even the rocks sit back, so wise,
Cracking their surfaces, finding surprise.
"Why not tell tales of the old mud pies,
Or how the beetle can dance and fly?"

In this garden where smiles do bloom,
Late blooms are raucous, chasing the gloom.
So breathe in the laughter, let nature sing,
In every green corner, the humor is king!

Syllables in Verdant Embrace

Leaves of green in tangled glee,
Whisper jokes, they dance with me.
Words like vines twist round the sun,
Nature laughs, our rhymes are fun.

Petals giggle in the breeze,
Syllables flutter like bees.
The garden blooms a playful tune,
Insects tap as if in June.

Roots beneath with mischief thrive,
Plotting pranks to keep us live.
Foliage rustles, what a jest,
Nature's laughter, we are blessed.

Sprouting rhymes both bright and bold,
Stories tangled, tales retold.
With every sprout, the humor blends,
In this garden, joy transcends.

Emerald Verses Unfurled

Bright green stems hold secrets rare,
Whispers wrapped in leafy air.
Each line blooms, a cheeky jest,
Nature's chaos, we are blessed.

Laughter echoes through the grove,
In each breath, the fun we wove.
Sprouts and rhymes, a silly sight,
Dancing shadows, pure delight.

Petals muse with sway and spin,
Jokes are sprouting from within.
A twist of leaf brings giggles wide,
In every turn, the joys abide.

Emerald verses, blooming loud,
Nature's whimsy, bold and proud.
In the garden, laughter's glare,
Woven words hang in the air.

Tangled Words and Tendrils

Vines entwined in comical chase,
Words collide, we lose our place.
Green delights, a twisting plot,
Laughter echoes, tangled tot.

With every twist, a pun appears,
Nature's jest through verdant years.
Roots connect like silly friends,
In this patch, the fun extends.

Petals blush with playful grin,
As they wink, the jokes begin.
Leaves confide in softer tones,
Tickling buds with leafy moans.

In this patchwork, joy's the aim,
Silly verses, wild and tame.
Tendrils laugh and stretch their reach,
In a world that loves to teach.

Rhythm of the Climbing Plant

Bouncing phrases climb the wall,
As laughter plays, we heed the call.
Each little vine stretches its joke,
In this green space, giggles provoke.

Rhythms sway with every breeze,
Leaves tap dance beneath the trees.
Nature's chorus sings of cheer,
In each rustle, joy draws near.

Sprouts parade with a jaunty flair,
Witty rhymes hang in the air.
Every curl, a story's mark,
In sunlight's glow, we leave a spark.

Climbing high, we twist and turn,
With every line, the fables churn.
A vibrant plant, a playful state,
In this rhythm, we celebrate.

Green Shadows on the Page

In the corner a vine does creep,
It whispers secrets, oh so deep.
With leaves like fingers, it reaches wide,
Where thoughts take root, and dreams collide.

A pencil dances, twirls around,
While leafy whispers make no sound.
The ink spills stories, wild and free,
As green conspirators, glee, and glee.

Bouncing off books, in playful glee,
Creating tales, just you and me.
The words tickle; they giggle and play,
In this garden of thoughts, we lose our way.

So let's write on, let humor reign,
With playful quirks, and no disdain.
For in this jungle of merriment spread,
The shadows of green bring laughter instead.

Blooms of Inspiration

There's a bloom on my desk, what a surprise,
With petals of whimsy dancing in the skies.
A thought pops up, like a daisy's cheer,
And writes itself in a voice we hear.

The colors splash, a riotous scene,
With humor wrapped in emerald green.
Each line a petal, soft and light,
In a garden where giggles take flight.

A wacky tale of when plants converse,
Revealing secrets in the universe.
Each word a bud, bursting with sound,
Chasing the mundane far from ground.

So come along, let's weave a song,
In this floral world where we both belong.
With laughter and joy, we'll sow the seeds,
Of whimsical stories where humor leads.

Leafy Allegories in Cadence

Beneath the leaves, a jest unfolds,
In every stem, a tale retold.
A rhyming vine, with a twist of fate,
Turns every scribble into something great.

Each leafy line does sway and sway,
A giggle here, a chuckle there play.
As metaphors dance like butterflies,
Tickling each thought like a silly surprise.

The cliche blooms in laughter's embrace,
With snickers and grins, we find our place.
In tangled verses, humor's delight,
Brings a smile to the dimmest of nights.

So we'll spin words till the sun goes down,
In this leafy circus, joy we crown.
For every leaf whispers 'just have fun',
In this strange world, we're never done.

Whispers Among the Vines

Sneaky tendrils twist and twine,
As laughter echoes through the vine.
Small giggles pop, like bubbles of cheer,
Words shimmy forth, drawing us near.

In the garden of lines, jokes grow tall,
With puns that tumble and occasionally fall.
A leafy chuckle or two for the road,
As rhymes take shape, and mirth explodes.

The sun sets low, casting shadows bright,
Where wit takes flight in the cool of night.
In this maze of green, we find delight,
As whispers among the vines take flight.

So gather 'round, let's share a laugh,
In this leafy realm, let's take a gaffe.
For humor grows wild, just like the breeze,
In the arms of nature, our minds find ease.

The Scribe of the Garden

In a corner, a vine takes pen,
Scrawling stories of flowers and men.
Leaves whisper tales in gentle breeze,
Chasing off boredom with eager tease.

A snail is the scribe's trusty mate,
Writing slow, but it's never too late.
Each droplet of dew, a word in cue,
Giggling gently, it's not just for few.

The sun winks down, a cheerful muse,
As ants dance around with quirky shoes.
Nature's laugh resonates so light,
Making mischief till the fall of night.

In every curl, a plot twist spins,
With critters known for silly sins.
The garden's stage, oh what a sight,
In this scribbling space, joy feels so right.

Nature's Literary Embrace

Sunlight drafts stories, warm and bright,
While shadows whisper secrets of the night.
Each blade of grass pens a silly quip,
As daisies and dandelions joyfully skip.

The brook babbles lines, cosmic and wide,
While frogs croak sonnets, in leaps they glide.
Leaves dance like poets, free in their craft,
A banquet of humor, nature's own draft.

Petals flutter with a cheeky grin,
Inviting each moment for laughter to spin.
Clouds float by with a ghostly cheer,
Imprisoning joy, it just can't disappear.

With a buzz and a chirp, the tales unfold,
In the arms of green, laughter grows bold.
Nature's embrace, a cozy delight,
Bringing forth smiles, all day and night.

Unfurled Lines of Life

Vines twist and twirl in playful jest,
Spinning out lyrics that never rest.
A caterpillar pens a memoir quite grand,
On leaves so green, each word's in demand.

With a wobble and giggle, the beetle arrives,
Adding verse with his rowdy high-fives.
The petals bloom in a raucous cheer,
Nature's party, oh so sincere!

Sunflowers pose, the stars of the show,
While wind carries tales where few dare to go.
A squirrel in denim writes lofty prose,
Climbing each branch, a poetic pose.

Whimsical beings, from bee to the fern,
Share insights and laughs, offering their turn.
In this garden of giggles, life's lines intertwine,
Celebrating existence, both yours and mine.

Verses in Verdancy

A leafy manuscript blossoms and grows,
While roots write secrets in supple flows.
Mushrooms chuckle, as rain starts to pour,
Bouncing in puddles, asking for more!

The crickets compose, night's serenade,
Tickling the grass with each lyric laid.
A gentle breeze carries the silly sound,
As laughter erupts from the greening ground.

With daisies giggling, and clovers in row,
Every plant wishes the world to know.
That the jigs of the day are a joyous feat,
In verdant spaces where humor's complete.

Under the moon, a poet's delight,
Crafting a stanza, all cozy and bright.
In this realm of green, laughter takes flight,
Transforming each moment into pure light.

Poetic Roots

In a pot where dreams might grow,
Words tangled like a wild toe.
They dance in the sunlight, oh so bright,
With laughter that tickles every night.

Leaves munch on phrases, what a treat,
A salad of jest, can't be beat.
They whisper secrets that make you chuckle,
As rhymes take root in a playful puzzle.

Watered with humor, a cheerful spray,
Growing lines that swing and sway.
In this garden of giggles and light,
Each word a sprout, so full of delight.

So let's grow verses, let them intertwine,
In the wildest fun, let's shine.
For every line has a smile in tow,
In this merry plantation, let's go!

The Feminine Vine

A lady vine climbs with such flair,
Twisting and turning without a care.
She's sassy, she's bold, she's here to please,
Laughing in the breeze, with playful ease.

In her curls, tales do entwine,
Witty remarks like sparkling wine.
She stretches high, touching the sky,
With a wink and a nod, oh me, oh my!

Dancing around the garden scene,
Her spirit is bright, her laughter keen.
With every twist, she steals the show,
In her leafy realm, watch her go!

Growing wild in every direction,
She roots for fun, her sole perfection.
With laughter blooming, she's fine and divine,
In this whimsical life, oh, what a vine!

Stanzas Under the Canopy

Beneath a leafy, verdant shade,
Stanzas gather like a parade.
Chasing giggles, spreading cheer,
In this vibrant realm, oh so dear.

Each leaf a line, so crisp and bright,
They tickle the air with pure delight.
With whispers of chuckles in the breeze,
Poems emerge as the mind's tease.

Beneath the canopy, shadows play,
Words like critters, darting away.
In laughter's embrace, they'll always dwell,
In this grove where banter swells.

So let the stanzas dance and sing,
Under the green, let joy take wing.
With every breath, let mirth ignite,
In this space where dreams feel right!

The Veins of Inspiration

In a jungle of jests, the veins run clear,
Flowing with laughter, bubbling with cheer.
Each twist and turn, a whimsical thought,
In the world of words, hilarity's caught.

They travel like rivers, carving the land,
Generating giggles, isn't it grand?
Inspiration springs from every creak,
With humor on tap, oh isn't that sleek?

Veins weave stories that tickle the mind,
A carnival of quirks, boldly aligned.
Where playful prose meets the art of fun,
In this raucous realm, there's joy for everyone!

So let's water the words with laughter's delight,
And nourish the roots with giggles, all night.
In the dance of ideas, let's all take part,
For the veins of inspiration are rich in art!

The Sylvan Sonnet

In a pot, a leafy friend,
Wanders thoughts that never end.
Whispers softly to the air,
Leaves like laughter, everywhere.

Nature's jest, a tangled vine,
Chatting 'bout the sun's design.
Roots that tickle, stems that tease,
Growing stories with such ease.

A twisty dance of green delight,
Sunbeams join the leafy fight.
Each glance brings a giggle, true,
Nature's humor shining through.

With every leaf, a tale unfolds,
Not in books but in the molds.
A shining leaf, a funny deed,
In this world, we plant the seed.

Reaching for the Line

Stretched out, a vine on the wall,
Reminds me to answer the call.
Jokes entwined in every leaf,
Offering both joy and grief.

A gentle tug, the leaves will sway,
Daring the sun, "Come out and play!"
With roots like jokes that dig so deep,
They burst awake from their sleep.

I scribble notes on scraps of air,
As sunlight plants its cheeky dare.
Words grow wild in laughter's shade,
Secrets in every twist we've made.

A green companion, sprightly and bright,
Sways and swirls in pure delight.
What rhymes can sprout from leafy dreams?
Nature giggles, or so it seems.

Words Wreathed in Nature

Woven whispers blend with light,
Textured tales take silly flight.
Leaves like letters, spilling down,
Nature bats her leafy crown.

Phrases float on gentle breeze,
Wishing for a world of cheese!
Each twist and turn, a laugh in bloom,
Filling up the sunny room.

With vines that twirl in playful games,
Telling tales without any names.
Each tiny leaf, a pun so sweet,
Nature's laughter, oh so neat!

In every petal, humor shines,
Between the jokes, the life aligns.
A tapestry of giggles spun,
In the arms of the golden sun.

Dreaming in Green

In my dreams, a jungle grows,
Funny stories in the prose.
Leaves are laughing, so they say,
Sprouting chuckles every day.

Roots are ticklish, stems like jokes,
Whispering secrets, nature pokes.
A tendril here, a zany shout,
Who knew the green could be so loud?

Dancing lightly in the breeze,
Sharing wisdom with such ease.
A leafy friend with giggling prance,
Round and round, we take a chance.

With each new sprout, the laughter flows,
In a world where joy just grows.
Tales of green in playful cheer,
Whisking wonder, far and near.

Written Under the Green Sky

Under the sky of leafy dreams,
My thoughts are tangled, bursting seams.
A vine that whispers, 'What's your plan?'
I'm still finding shoes to fit my van.

Each twist and turn, a giggle flows,
Like plants that dance with silly toes.
A pot of ink, a blooper line,
I water words with jokes divine.

In a garden where puns entwine,
The sunlight winks, and I can't whine.
A seedling's laugh, the breeze's cheer,
I write my rhymes for all to hear.

A Palette of Growth

With every leaf, a color bright,
I mix my thoughts, a playful sight.
A dash of giggle, a splash of fun,
The canvas beams, my work begun.

I paint in strokes of morning cheer,
Each line a bloom that wants to steer.
The laughter sprouts between the hues,
In every shade, a joke ensues.

A palette rich, a quirky blend,
Where humor's roots and rhymes extend.
With every brush, my heart does sway,
Crafting joy from night to day.

Leaves and Lines

Leaves unfurl like jokes in air,
Spreading laughter, light, and flair.
A scribbled note upon each green,
A punning leaf, a playful scene.

In corners where the sunlight beams,
I twine my thoughts in joyful dreams.
Each line a twist, a funny turn,
A leaf that giggles, waiting to learn.

With every branch, a story grows,
Ink drips like rain, and off it goes!
The wind will laugh, the paper curls,
As I weave lines with leafy swirls.

The Canvas of Climbing Thoughts

Thoughts creep up like vines in spring,
A canvas full of giggles zing.
They stretch for laughs, they twist and weave,
In every corner, a joke conceived.

With climbing lines and bouncing glee,
I plant my puns for all to see.
The height of humor, rich and wide,
Where every joke can freely glide.

A ladder made of dreams and cheer,
I snip away my doubts and fear.
Each sentence clings, a leafy thread,
As laughter blooms within my head.

The Prose of Perseverance

In a pot sat a vine, so spry,
Twisting round like a circus guy.
Each leaf a story, a laughter ring,
In daylight's glow, they dance and sing.

With water splashed, it took a chance,
Broke all the norms in a leafy dance.
Roots tangled like a messy hair,
Still, it sprouted without a care.

A sunbeam winked, a cheeky tease,
Wrote notes on leaves, aiming to please.
It whispered tales from up above,
As the world beneath grew softer, in love.

Through ups and downs, it stayed so bold,
With twists and tales yet to be told.
In a crazy world, it found its way,
Rooted in laughter, come what may.

Whispers from the Green Shadows

In a corner, green leaves conspire,
Plotting mischief, we all admire.
With giggles wrapped in every curl,
They tickle the air in a leafy whirl.

A shadow dances on the wall,
As ivy giggles at each fall.
Reaching out with cheeky flair,
It greets the sunlight, without a care.

The pots are full of clever quirks,
Each one has tricks, it really works!
The more you stare, the fun you find,
Green whispers playing tricks on the mind.

And when you water, oh what a scene,
Leaves high-five in a joyful green.
With every drop, they cheer and sway,
In shadows deep, they laugh and play.

A Symphony of Shades

A foliage orchestra plays in tune,
With leaves like notes, under the moon.
They rustle softly, a comedic show,
Playing tunes that only they know.

The sunlight's rays, a spotlight bright,
As green performers take their flight.
Each vine a solo, a giggle here,
Creating laughter, making it clear.

Oh, the colors, a vibrant jest,
In nature's hall, they rise and rest.
When autumn leaves choose to retreat,
The stalks still dance, never miss a beat.

A harmony that grows and bends,
In this garden, joy never ends.
For in the shades, laughter's the key,
A symphony of green, wild and free.

The Blooming Lines

Lines curled like a playful vine,
With petals bright, they intertwine.
Each bloom a joke, a cheeky grin,
In nature's story, we all win.

The gardener chuckles, hands in dirt,
Spreading joy with every sprurt.
With every seed, a giggle's sown,
In blooming lines, laughter's grown.

Chasing sunlight, oh what a chase,
Flowers sprouting in a race.
Their colors burst, a jester's show,
As petals play and laughter flows.

So here's to the blooms of every hue,
A merry band with a point of view.
In every garden, the cheer aligns,
With joy blossoming in blooming lines.

The Spirit of the Leaf

In a pot so snug and bright,
A leafy friend, a pure delight.
It leans to sip the morning dew,
Whispers secrets, just for you.

With cheeky curls that twist and sway,
It dances in the sun's warm ray.
Each new shoot a curious peek,
A green comedian, so to speak.

As shadows stretch, it tells a joke,
About the plants, their leafy folk.
"Why did I climb? To see the sky!"
With laughter, makes the hours fly.

So raise a toast to leafy cheer,
To our flowing friend, we hold dear.
In every twist, a playful tease,
Nature's humor brings us ease.

Echoes of the Climbing Vine

A twisty vine that wants to hug,
It's got ambition, snug as a bug.
With every inch, it climbs with glee,
"Higher and higher!" it shouts to me.

It reaches for each dizzy height,
With leafy arms, it takes to flight.
For every wall that's cold and bare,
It adds a smile and some flair.

"Watch out!" it says, "I might just grow,
Into your hair—just letting you know!"
A playful tease, a leafy prank,
A green comedian with a wank.

So let it twist your frown away,
Nature's giggle in the sunlight's play.
In its embrace, there's room to shine,
An echo of joy, a fun design.

Verses in the Canopy

Beneath a leafy, dancing shade,
Where laughter's grown and joy is made.
Each branch a poet, every leaf,
A verse to spark, a sweet relief.

With rustling words and gentle rants,
They flirt and play, the leafy plants.
"Why write in soil? Let's tell it here!"
A chorus cracks, a happy cheer.

Each sunbeam beams, a laughing rhyme,
As vines craft tales that cross through time.
Charming critters join the fun,
Cocooning plots till day is done.

In nature's plot, each line a thread,
Of giggles spun from what was said.
So sip the air, let laughter flow,
In leafy tales where giggles grow.

Nature's Textual Harmony

In every leaf, a tale unfolds,
With humor stitched in green and gold.
"What rhymes with leaf? A funny grief!"
It cackles loud, our leafy chief.

With every twist, a witty quip,
It teaches us to laugh and flip.
A vine that writes with every curl,
A jester in the plant world swirl.

When rain arrives, it sings, "Oh yay!
A splash of fun to brighten the day!"
It shakes off drops, a joyful dance,
A playful troupe, given the chance.

So raise a glass to nature's jest,
In blooms and leaves we find our best.
Let's laugh with greens, in leafy rhyme,
For nature's charm transcends all time.

Lush Vines of Verse

In a garden where rhymes entwine,
The leaves tickle thoughts, so divine.
They wrap around jokes, quite cheeky,
As laughter blooms, oh so freaky.

Each line a tendril, reaching wide,
Hiding puns where secrets bide.
Flipping metaphors like a vine,
Whispering jokes with a twist of brine.

The scribbles dance in joyous haste,
Mischief mingles with the paste.
Petals drip with comic flare,
Bursting forth from leafy lair.

Nature's gift, both bright and wild,
Fooling each and every child.
They laugh as laughter finds its way,
In this green world where words sway.

Whispered Leaves in Stanza

Leafy whispers paint the page,
Each word an actor on the stage.
With leafy giggles, they conspire,
Telling tales that never tire.

In shadows where the sunlight plays,
Banter blooms in clever ways.
Stanzas twist and vines they climb,
Crafting humor, one line at a time.

Caterpillars swap silly lore,
Twirling tales from door to door.
Chasing butterflies of glee,
Finding joy in words set free.

A leaf may fall, a pun may land,
As laughter shakes the poet's hand.
So plant your thoughts, let giggles birth,
In whispered leaves, discover mirth.

Growth Beneath the Ink

Underneath this inked expanse,
Roots of laughter twist and dance.
Jokes sprout up like wildflowers,
In this pot, humor empowers.

As verses climb, they tickle the air,
Silly seedlings beyond compare.
Nourished by thoughts, funny and bright,
They reach for joy, bask in the light.

The water of wit flows evergreen,
In the soil of dreams, nothing is mean.
A pun here, a quip there,
Each line brings giggles, beyond compare.

Unruly vines of vibrant jest,
In the garden of thought, they're the best.
So let them grow, oh let them sing,
For laughter is the finest spring.

Green Grapes of Expression

Bunches of words hang in the sun,
Fruity phrases, oh what fun!
They pop like bubbles, so sweet and spry,
Each giggle deeper than the sky.

The vine of humor twists and bends,
Carrying laughter to all it sends.
Picked with care, these jesters shine,
Juicy and ripe, a true goldmine.

In this orchard of silly lines,
Chortles entwine like playful vines.
Grapes of wit, a luscious treat,
Tasting joy with every beat.

So raise a glass, let giggles flow,
For in each grape, there's a hearty glow.
Cheers to the words that dance and play,
In the vineyard of laughter, seize the day!

Serpentine Stanzas

In a pot so big, it dreams of the sky,
A leaf gives a wink, and I can't help but sigh.
It coils and it twirls, like a dancer in glee,
"A vine or a snake? You decide, my friend, see!"

With a twist and a turn, it wraps tight around,
My pencil's now tangled, in verdant profound.
"Poems should flourish!" it whispers with cheer,
But all I can think of is how to steer clear.

A tumble, a fumble, my words now in knots,
This plant's not a muse, but it ties up my thoughts.
I giggle and laugh, as it sprawls on the floor,
"Is this art or a mess?" I can't be sure anymore.

So here's to the vine, decorator of prose,
With a trickster's charm, it just goes where it goes.
I'll call it my guide through the commas and quips,
A landscape of chaos, with leafy dance tips.

Rhymes from the Rainforest

In the jungle so green, there's a poet so sly,
With a tap of a toe, and a gleam in the eye.
Each leaf that he sees laughs and whispers away,
"Let's rhyme all the critters, and join in the fray!"

A sloth with a hat, and a parrot that croaks,
Join in on the fun, with their giggliest jokes.
"What do you call vines that just won't align?"
"Tangled relationships, but we're doing just fine!"

The monkeys swing low, and the flowers all sway,
The stories unfold in a zany ballet.
Each verse tells a tale, with a chuckle or two,
As frogs in the reeds echo, "Ribbit! It's true!"

So tiptoe along, through this riot of green,
Where laughter and words mix, like a vibrant cuisine.
In the rainforest's heart, with a shimmy and smirk,
You'll find that the joy of the verses will work.

Sonnet of the Spiraling Leaf

Oh, a leaf with a twist, how it frolics about,
It spirals and giggles, with no hint of doubt.
With a flourish and flip, it beckons me near,
"Join in this dance, let's erase all the fear!"

A rhymed rotation, like a grand spinning wheel,
It tickles my senses, oh what a surreal feel!
"Why be straightforward, when you can just swirl?"
This plant has a point—let's give it a whirl!

It stretches its arms, like a comical star,
"Roses may be red, but what's with a jar?"
My rhyme takes a plunge, in the vine's joyful sea,
As I laugh with each turn, set my wild thoughts free.

So here's to the leaf with its whimsical twist,
A sonnet that dances, and I can't resist.
With each playful curl, it spins merrily bright,
In lush leafy laughter, my words take to flight.

Verses Woven in Green

Between pots and petals, the humor is thick,
A garden of giggles, where vines play a trick.
"Why did the orchid refuse to wear shoes?"
"It wanted to root, in its own little muse!"

The stems all entwined, they conspire at dusk,
With whispers and winks, it's a plot full of husk.
"What do you call leaves when they start to complain?"
"Drama queens of the foliage, always in pain!"

With laughter and quirks, my words sprout and grow,
In this leafy abode, where mischief can flow.
"A haiku for bugs?" they chirp with delight,
As fireflies flicker, and dance through the night.

So raise a green glass to the quirks of the shrub,
For laughter and wit, form a leafy love club.
With each verse I sow, in this garden of cheer,
The poetry blooms, as the silliness nears.

Melodies of the Understory

In the jungle of dreams, leaves take a twist,
They giggle and dance, oh, don't they insist?
A vine whispers jokes to the sun with a grin,
While bugs harmonize under the ferns' gentle spin.

A lizard narrates tales, tail curling tight,
Of how he once danced with a butterfly's flight.
Frogs join in laughter, a comical choir,
Their croaks are the echoes of silliness higher.

The shadows, they tease, as daylight grows dim,
Oh, watch out for branches that tickle on a whim!
With laughter and light, the foliage sways,
It's a party beneath, where the wacky life plays.

So raise up your cups, made of acorn and bark,
To the leafy companions that brighten the dark.
In the layers of green, where the wild critters roam,
Every twist of a stem sings, "Welcome to home!"

Shadows and Silhouettes

The clay pots dance, as if stored with delight,
Embodying joy in the warm, fuzzy light.
Leaves laugh together, a cheeky duet,
While crickets provide a rhythmic vignette.

Stems stretch and bend, in a silly parade,
Oh, watch them all turbo, don't be dismayed!
With every soft rustle, a pun comes alive,
As roots play hopscotch and branches high-five.

Curtains of green frame a hilarious view,
Where squirrels do pirouettes, acorns in queue.
Laughter cascades as shadows cling tight,
To the silly ballet that thrives in the night.

A chorus of leaves presents their grand show,
In this lively abode, full of giggles and glow.
So tip your hats to the green that won't quit,
Join in the fun, just don't get hit!

Lush Inspirations

In the forest of whimsy, where giggles grow tall,
A plant in a pot thinks it's leading the ball.
Leaves bob up and down, in a frolicsome fashion,
Creating a scene of delightful impassion.

With dust bunnies' laughter, they tickle the ground,
As shrubs play charades, in their rustling sound.
A sunflower grins at a rose with a wink,
Together they plot all the mischief they think.

The air fills with wonders, as vines weave and spin,
While mushrooms compose symphonies, thin.
A giggling toadstool joins the little fun crew,
With gooey punchlines made just for you!

So wander through green where the laughter is free,
And let your heart revel in nature's decree.
A bulbous broccoli leads the wacky parade,
In this garden of joy, let your worries slide fade.

Echoing in the Greenery

Beneath the wide leaf that sways like a hat,
Worms whisper secrets while teasing the cat.
The daisies are flirts, prancing in style,
As bees buzz their tunes, making the world smile.

A pumpkin counts stars, but forgot how to cheer,
While shadows do jigs on the soil's cozy sphere.
Fronds sway with laughter, casting a spell,
As petals tell stories, each one is a bell!

Calm breezes bounce through with quips in their tails,
As the roots hold a meeting, exchanging their tales.
With twirls and with sways, the garden's a jig,
Where even the weeds do a wobbly gig.

So stroll through this place, where the giggles abound,
In the giggling greens, let your heart stick around.
Each bud and each leaf conveys a sweet rhyme,
In the lush of the green, there's always good time!

Nature's Quill Entwined

In a garden, leaves sway and caper,
With whispers of mischief, they play the paper.
Bugs scribble notes in the morning light,
While squirrels type tales on a branch in flight.

A beetle in glasses, a poet in tow,
Recites all his poems to the flowers below.
The daisies all giggle, the sunflowers chime,
As they clap their green hands, saving pennies and thyme.

Vines twist and turn, forming letters above,
Sending messages tangled with laughter and love.
The wind holds the quill and scribbles a tune,
While the sun paints the pages with rays of monsoon.

So if ever you wander through nature's rich plot,
Just listen, take note of the stories they've got.
For every bold vine sprawls a tale that includes,
The humor in growing, in friendship, and foods.

Sonnet of the Twining Stems

Two stems entwined in a tangled embrace,
Giggle and wiggle in a leafy race.
One says, "You're knotting, not keeping it cool!"
The other quips back, "You're the fool here, the fool!"

"Let's dance!" shouts the fern with leaves open wide,
The bamboo nods slowly, saying, "I'll glide!"
With laughter like rustling through branches so spry,
They twirl and they spin, while the crickets all sigh.

"Your roots are too knotted, they resemble a braid,"
Yelled a nearby cactus, jealousy displayed.
"Our twine is much better," responded the sage,
"Come here and behold our magnificent page."

So stems continue their grand comic scheme,
A sonnet of humor, their botanical dream.
In this leafy theater, together they rhyme,
As nature's odd jesters, they frolic in time.

Inked Leaves and Breezy Rhyme

In the forest, leaves pen poems on air,
With a quirk of the wind, they swirl without care.
Dandelions giggle and scatter their seeds,
While the willow tree doodles in shades of green weeds.

A grasshopper hops in a rhythmic beat,
Sketching his verses while tapping his feet.
"Oh look," shouts a crow, "proud artist, I see!
Create me a sonnet with rhyme and with glee."

The daisies assist with their petals bright white,
Unraveling puns under moon's silver light.
With each sudden gust, new verses appear,
As the trees shake their branches and cheer with good cheer.

Inked leaves laugh softly, drumming in time,
Their thoughts swaying freely, escaping the grime.
So gather your joy from this green, breezy height,
For every sweet whisper brings laughter and light.

Flourishing Words Under Canopy

Beneath the vast leaves of the expansive sky,
The whispers of nature engage in a sly.
"That branch is too low," a grumpy old oak,
Said to a vine who had tangled his cloak.

A bumblebee buzzed, with words like confetti,
"Don't mope, dear old friend, come dance! It's quite petty."
The petals exploded with colors so bright,
As laughter erupted, from morning till night.

A squirrel with glasses recited his prose,
With a twitch of his tail and a flair in his toes.
"Oh nature," he chirped, "you're a wonder to see,
Transforming each moment into whimsical spree!"

So under the canopy of dreams intertwined,
Flourishing words tell tales that are kind.
In the shade and the sun, life dances and streams,
Where the roots and the leaves share the funniest dreams.

An Ode to Climbing Green

In corners they creep with a smile,
Reaching for sunlight all the while.
A twist, a turn, a leafy delight,
Scaring the cat in the depth of night.

They climb up bookshelves, defy all rules,
Making mockeries of our old-school tools.
With vibrant leaves in a verdant mess,
Who knew houseplants could bring such stress?

A villain in waiting, they play their part,
Hiding my keys like a masterful art.
In the battle of space, they'll surely win,
As I navigate tissues and toys within.

Yet still, they bring laughter with each new sprout,
Bantering with roommates, there's never a drought.
With a chuckle and grin, I watch them grow,
What characters they are, putting on a show!

Tonal Tendrils

In my lounge they sway, those leafy things,
Singing ballads of growth on invisible strings.
They tangle and twist in a merry old dance,
Inviting the dust bunnies to join in the prance.

A comedian's dream, they mimic my style,
Drooping down low with a cheeky smile.
Mocking my focus while I'm on a call,
As I fumble for words and nearly fall.

They boast of their heights while I'm sitting low,
Taking my space like they steal the show.
With leafy applause, they cheer on my plight,
In a comedy club beneath the moonlight.

Whispering secrets as I tiptoe by,
Their antics keep me giggling, oh my, oh my!
In this jungle of silence, they thrive with glee,
The funniest mates, they sure are to me!

The Art of Growth

With a sip of water, they grow on their way,
Making it look easy, like kids at play.
Stretching so tall with a grin on each leaf,
While I trip over pots, oh what a relief!

Dress up the corner, that's their grand plan,
They're thriving like pros, I'm their biggest fan.
In the middle of chaos, they steal the crowd,
Dressed up in green, they scream it out loud!

I'm tangled in deadlines, they're tangling too,
Making life interesting with every new hue.
In this dance of life, I lead with my heart,
While these sprightly greens steal the best part.

They jive and they bop in the light of the sun,
Planting their laughter, and oh, what fun!
With every new leaf, what a masterpiece,
They remind me to smile, relax, and cease!

Petals and Prose

In the realm of words, where I often dwell,
My leafy companions know me so well.
They speak without sound, with whispers and sighs,
Each new little shoot is a sweet surprise.

They tell me their tales of the sun's warm embrace,
While I type away, lost in this race.
With stories of growth and dreams that they weave,
How can I write when they're hard to believe?

A leaf on the table, a vine on my chair,
Together creating a splash everywhere.
Between cups of coffee and mess of my notes,
They're growing their way into all of my quotes.

In the laughter of life, in the shade of the trees,
These green little jesters float with the breeze.
What fun they provide in my wild little prose,
Turning words into joy, blooming thoughts as they rose!

The Whispering Vines

In the garden, whispers flow,
Leaves converse, secrets grow.
A vine stretched high, looking down,
Said the flower, "Stop that frown!"

Laughter twines between the stems,
Petals dance like cherished gems.
Nature's jokes, a sight to see,
Even critters chuckle with glee!

Tangled roots with stories old,
Vines laugh at the bold and cold.
A snail said, "Gonna race you all!"
But ended up just taking a crawl!

In every leaf, a chuckle found,
As they wiggle on the ground.
Nature's humor, wild and free,
Whispering joy in harmony.

Inked Leaves

On sheets of green, we scribble fate,
With petals bright, we decorate.
An artist squirrel, furrily deft,
Drew a picture, and oh, what a heft!

The ink ran wild, a messy spree,
With drips and drops from a busy bee.
"Call this one 'The Buzzing Blush!'"
While nearby, a tumbleweed made a rush.

A chubby ladybug, with flair,
Wrote love notes in the fragrant air.
While flowers giggled at the sight,
"Her lines are cute, but not quite right!"

With every breeze, the jokes took flight,
Pollen puns hang in daylight.
Each leaf a canvas, bold and spry,
Turning laughter into a butterfly.

A Garden of Stanzas

In rows of blooms, the verses grow,
Colors burst in playful show.
A daisy rhymes with dandelion,
While tulips hum a silly lion.

The hedgehog recites, in a slow, sweet tone,
But stutters at the word 'alone!'
Butterflies flutter, taking the stage,
Spinning tales that amuse and engage.

A grasshopper led a chorus high,
With crickets chirping, "Oh me, oh my!"
A joke so funny it made leaves sway,
"Did you hear the weed say, 'I'd like to stay'?"

Petals burst with giggles loud,
Chasing clouds, each one proud.
A garden filled with laughter's twang,
Creating magic with every clang.

Climbing Thoughts in Lush Corners

In the corners where the shadows play,
Ideas climb in a silly way.
A vine climbed up to grab a star,
And said, "I'm off to be a czar!"

Beneath the leaves, thoughts twist and wind,
Tickled by dreams they often find.
A worm wrote tales of long lost days,
With punchlines that will make you blaze!

Laughter echoes from the boughs,
As squirrels debate who runs the house.
"Oh, what a riot, do you see?"
The trees whisper, "We'll all agree!"

In these lush corners, joy will sprout,
Where silliness is what it's all about.
So climb along with every thought,
Finding humor in the garden sought.

Climbing Thoughts in Bloom

Thoughts creep up like vines in spring,
 Twisting 'round each word I bring.
They giggle as they stretch and sway,
 Crafting rhymes in a playful way.

A leaf whispers secrets to the breeze,
 Making meanings with such ease.
Chasing sunshine, they dance in glee,
 Words prance 'round like bees at tea.

Ideas sprout from roots so deep,
 While puns and giggles start to leap.
A garden of humor, verdant and bright,
 Growing laughter both day and night.

So here's to scribbles, wild and free,
 With each twist, they create a spree.
Climbing thoughts in bloom today,
 A poetic romp, come out and play!

Fragrant Lines and Tendrils

Lines unfurl like fragrant blooms,
Entangled in garden grooms.
Tendrils twirl with comic flair,
They tickle thoughts in mid-air.

Each stanza sprouts with clever jest,
A vine of laughter, never rest.
Words entwine in jolly jest,
A verbal game, let's be the best.

In sunlight's grace, they sway and tease,
Chasing giggles with fervent ease.
Oh, that rhyme, it steals the scene,
Like playful plants, so fresh and green.

So gather 'round and share a laugh,
In fragrant lines, we'll pen our path.
With every twist, let joy ignite,
In this garden of delight!

The Language of Lushness

In the garden of giggles, I find my voice,
The lushness of laughter, a happy choice.
Each leaf a word, each root a rhyme,
Blooming hilarity, it's our time.

Words scatter 'round like playful seeds,
Sprouting smiles, fulfilling needs.
With every chuckle, the lines expand,
In this rich jungle, we make our stand.

The sun peeks through, a winking eye,
With meandering lines, we lift so high.
Lushness speaks in comedy's tune,
Planting joy beneath the moon.

So let's dance where the wild thoughts grow,
In fields of green where laughter flows.
Ancient rhythms in vibrant play,
With the language of lushness, we'll stay!

Roots of Rhyme and Reflection

Burrowing deep, where jokes take root,
Rhyme and reflection, a sturdy boot.
Digging for humor beneath the ground,
Where roots of laughter are always found.

With every twist of the wordy vine,
Reflecting life with a silly line.
In the soil of thought, we plant our jokes,
Fertile ground where laughter pokes.

Mirthy mirages dance in the shade,
Learning to laugh, we're not afraid.
Rooted in joy, we share our plight,
In the garden of giggles, we take flight.

So let's harvest joy, one line at a time,
With roots of rhyme in perfect chime.
Reflection grows in laughter's grace,
As we cultivate a cheerful space.

Metaphors in Mulch

In the garden of wit, I dig and plant,
Where puns grow strong and ants hold a chant.
With each shovelful, humor blooms and spreads,
My daisies tell jokes, while tulips make beds.

The soil's a canvas, muddy and bright,
As I mix in laughter, a comical sight.
There's mirth in the weeds, a chuckle in roots,
Where every old spade seems to wear funny boots.

Gardening gloves spotted with giggles and grime,
I weave silly tales, turn each chore into rhyme.
With every sprout singing a wry nursery tune,
I laugh with the breezes beneath the full moon.

So join me, my friend, in this lively jest,
Where flora and laughter grow and invest.
We'll plant a few smiles in rows right and left,
In this patch of delight, we garden, bereft.

The Green-Swirled Canvas

Oh, the paintbrush is green, a wild, vibrant hue,
With each stroke, I chuckle at things that I view.
Swirls of mischief dance on the arbor's tall bough,
As snickering leaves throw a party right now.

The trellis invites with an artful embrace,
Every branch is a burst of nature's old grace.
The vines twist and twirl, as if in a jest,
Creating a tale where green's truly blessed.

Butterflies flutter, sporting laughs on their wings,
While ladybugs join in with their fanciful flings.
Each petal a giggle, each stem a bright quip,
In this merry garden, let's take a fun trip.

As sunlight spills laughter upon every tile,
Nature's framed humor makes every heart smile.
With a palette of joy, we splash color anew,
In this whimsical world, there's magic for you.

Cadences of the Climbing Plant

Climbing high with glee, a twisty delight,
Leaving trails of giggles in the morning light.
Chasing after clouds, I bound like a vine,
Each step's a pun, each leaf a punchline.

The lattice of laughs grows sturdy and bold,
While tendrils of merriment in sunshine unfold.
I dance with the raindrops, hop up on a whim,
As vines curl and cavort, letting joy flow in.

In this rhythm of roots, every bud rings a bell,
Where the soil sways gently, and stories do swell.
I string up my jokes on the branches that grow,
With humor entwined, let the world bask in glow.

So climb with me, friend, where the laughter ignites,
In this splendid garden, up high in the heights.
Let's twine our thoughts together, let giggles ascend,
In the symphony of growth, we blossom, my friend.

Painted Leaf Reflections

In the mirror of nature, colors collide,
Leaves paint reflections, where humor resides.
Bright yellows and greens, a comedic parade,
Winking at passersby, chasing woes far away.

Each leaf a playwright, a performer so keen,
Whispers of laughter in shades of bright green.
The rustle of foliage, a delightful show,
Holding audience captive, as wild breezes blow.

Oh, the branches weave tales of folly and fun,
In the fabric of foliage, joy is never done.
The mirror of nature reflects every grin,
With every rustling leaf, a giggle begins.

So gaze at the portraits, the painted displays,
Where humor unfurls in the sunlight's warm rays.
In this park of reflections, let's dance in our shoes,
Embracing the laughter that every leaf cues.

Ink and Ivy

In a pot sat a vine, so bold,
With leaves like a story, yet untold.
It crept up the wall with a wiggly flair,
Spilling its secrets without a care.

The paintbrush met soil in a curious dance,
While the ivy just giggled, waiting its chance.
"I'll climb to the top, you write me a tale,
Together we'll flourish, we can't ever fail!"

With ink on the page and a twist of a vine,
They penned down the chaos, a tale so divine.
The drips and the drops made a splashy delight,
As ivy wrote verses that sparkled at night.

So here's to the green and the words that we sow,
In gardens of laughter where wild tales flow.
Let's raise a glass high to this whimsical team,
For ink and green leaves make a colorful dream.

The Heart of the Climbing Plant

In the corner stood a plant, quite spry,
Tangled with tales, reaching for the sky.
With twists and turns, it played peek-a-boo,
Swaying and laughing, it beckoned you too.

"What's better than rhymes with a side of green?"
It called out to poets, all hushed and serene.
"Let's climb up the walls of convention's gap,
And plant all our dreams in this leafy trap!"

It stretched and it reached for the bright afternoon,
While scribes brought their pens like a theme park tune.
With a touch of the absurd, they crafted each line,
While giggles erupted as words intertwined.

As the heart of the plant found its rhythm and beat,
The poets all danced on their wobbly feet.
"Join in our chorus, this vine is our chance,
To weave words like ivy in a comical dance!"

So let leafy laughter be the root of our art,
For humor and green grow from the same heart.
In the gardens of whimsy where chaos takes flight,
The heart of a climber shines brilliantly bright.

Lines from the Lush Depths

In the lushest depths where mischief resides,
A plant pens the story of whimsical tides.
With leaves made of laughter and vines made of fun,
It spills all its secrets beneath the warm sun.

"Come write me a tale, let's blend roots and rhymes,
We'll weave through the pages, transcending all times!"
The breeze held a chuckle, the sun winked its eye,
As words flew like petals that danced through the sky.

The shadows grew longer, yet still they would play,
Each line turned to mischief in a cheerful ballet.
A hiccup of joy twisted tightly in knots,
As the rhymes wrapped around like mischievous plots.

So let's frolic through phrases, like leaves through the air,

With each silly sentence, let's lighten the care.
For in these green realms where the laughter resounds,
We'll pen all the quirks that our quirkiness found!

In the depths of the lush, where absurdity grows,
Each line is a treasure that joyously flows.
With every new phrase, we find riotous cheer,
As ink drips with laughter—oh, what a grand year!

Written in the Garden's Embrace

In a garden so bright with a sprinkle of cheer,
Lived a quirky old plant with stories to share.
It stretched out its limbs, like arms wide and free,
Inviting the poets beneath its green tree.

With pens in their hands and a twinkle in eye,
They jotted down laughter as clouds drifted by.
"Join in the fun, let's frolic and play,
With roots in the soil, we'll dance night and day!"

The blooms burst with color, the sun shining wide,
As the scribes spun their yarns, their imaginations tied.
Each sentence took flight like a butterfly dream,
In a garden where giggles full of grace seemed to beam.

So come weave with the leaves, let the stories ignite,
Mirth woven through every word, oh what a sight!
For written in laughter, under branches so grand,
Lies the magic of verse, the joy of a band.

Henceforth, in this haven where whimsy takes root,
With the garden's embrace, it's a riot, to boot!
Let's roll in the lines of this playful affair,
Forever entwined in the light-hearted air!

www.ingramcontent.com/pod-product-compliance
Lightning Source LLC
Chambersburg PA
CBHW072217070526
44585CB00015B/1381